**ANCHOR BOOKS**

OF SENTIMENTAL VALUE

Edited by

Rachael Radford

First published in Great Britain in 2003 by
ANCHOR BOOKS
Remus House,
Coltsfoot Drive,
Peterborough, PE2 9JX
Telephone (01733) 898102

HB ISBN 1 84418 158 8
SB ISBN 1 84418 159 6

FOREWORD

Anchor Books is a small press, established in 1992, with the aim of promoting readable poetry to as wide an audience as possible.

We hope to establish an outlet for writers of poetry who may have struggled to see their work in print.

The poems presented here have been selected from many entries, and as always editing proved to be a difficult task.

I trust this selection will delight and please the authors and all those who enjoy reading poetry.

Rachael Radford
Editor

CONTENTS

MEMORIES OF YOU
(Dedicated to my grandson, Gary J Watson 22.4.85 - 22.10.01)

I know you've gone, but yet you're here,
I can feel you very near.
I can't reach out and touch,
I want to so very much.

My memories are all I've got,
And of those I've such a lot.
Good days, happy days sometimes sad,
But I'm grateful for what we had.

Every waking day a tear will spill,
It hurts so much, it always will.
You went without a kiss or goodbye,
No one knew you were going to die.

Although my heart is full of pain,
I know someday we will meet again.
I will always love you ever
And most of all forget you never.

Audrey Watson

WHERE HAVE ALL THE OLD WAYS GONE?

No bantams around the stackyard,
With fluffy black and yellow chicks,
No sow or baconers in the sty,
So there's no crowdie to mix.

No bacon to be salted,
And no cream to be churned,
Where have all the old ways gone,
To whatever have we turned?

Just a vast expanse like a prairie,
Devoid of hedges and trees,
Where acres of golden barley and wheat,
Gently sway their heads in the breeze.

No guinea fowl to tell of strangers,
No geese to chase them on their way,
No ducks on the pond,
Even that's not here today.

There's few men who can thatch a stack,
Or build a tattie pie,
Or hoe or snag turnips,
Or stand a stook to dry.

No heavy horses in the pasture,
No goats tethered in the lane,
No cockerels on the stubble
To glean the fallen grain.

No house cow in the byre,
No pet lambs to be fed,
Just a pile of receipts from the contractors,
And a big tractor in the shed.

E D Bowen

REALITY RESTORED

I hurried from the bookshop, package under arm
Feeling I had fallen under the author's charm
I close the front door firmly, the world left behind
Curled up by the fire with my precious find
Working through the pages, I enter another place
Where love and kindness were part of the human race
It was oh! so lovely to read a tale like this
Of a time of all the nice things so sadly missed
I sigh with satisfaction as I reach the last page
Wishing I didn't have to leave this bygone age
A tap at the door brings me to my feet
Grudgingly I open it, a smiling face I meet
'I'm so glad I found you,' the scruffy young man said
'Or I wouldn't have felt easy in my bed
You left this in the bookshop, it's got so much inside'
He handed me my wallet, red face trying to hide
I took his hands in mine with a grateful, humble heart
Much more than my wallet, this young man was able to impart
Let's not be hasty in judgement to the world around
For something I had lost, today I have found.

Veronica Quainton

IN MY SLEEP

It takes a very long time to heal
Your past, so painful was really real
Disconnected, a lifetime shut off
The black side of you, how it would scoff
Never happy, weren't sure why
Saw people cry but never I
Wrong you see, was taught that way
Abuse, it helped fill their day
Now though, decades on, what a waste
I see that child, I reach in haste
So do I dare rescue her, hold her hand
Do I dare help her to understand
That she was loved, if only by me
Do you think years on she could see
That she is worthy, as good as the rest
She is probably one of the best
Slowly, one step at a time
I want that child to see she's mine
The child within me, oh yes I care
I want to reach inside but do I dare
So much rejection along life's way
But no more, I don't do things that way
So come, let us at last be one
Today our whole life has begun
We'll struggle, we'll fall but we'll get there
All the pain of the past together we'll share
A happy life is waiting ahead
Instead of this life, where half of me is dead
To become whole, how good that could be
Instead of only being half of me
So I'll travel this road, I'll find that little girl
Then together we'll go forward, I know we will
So wish me luck, it takes courage to go so deep
But I've met her already, she came in my sleep

Sue Starling

Blood, Sweat and Tears

Think, just think, of all the blood, sweat and tears,
London has shed with the passing of years,
The dirt, dust and smog, the noise and the grime,
Poverty, slavery, squalor and crime.

Ambitions and hopes, mad schemings and fears,
Disease, depravity, vice, wines and beers,
Arts and culture can pass the test of time,
City of contrast from base to sublime.

Historical monuments, long endears,
Symbolise prestige of people and peers,
Noise of the traffic and church bells still chime,
Rags next to riches, cultures rise from slime.

Millions of people have lived, worked and died,
London remembers few only with pride.

S M Robertson

GOLDEN CHILDHOOD

Lollipops, barley sugar and candyfloss twirls,
Cornets of strawberry ice cream,
Daring helter-skelter and carnival horses,
Hall of mirrors where we'd shout and scream.
Roll your pennies or catch a fish,
Buy your ticket and enjoy the rides,
Roundabouts, dodgem cars and the penny arcade,
Try the swings, roller coaster and the slides.
Hours we'd spend at the beach funfair,
My brother, my cousins and me,
Thank God for golden childhood days,
Poignant memories - sunny and carefree.

Jean Mackenzie

A Message To Brian From Dave

Look back, my man, if you will, look back in time with me
Look back for almost sixty years and tell me what you see.
Do you see old Dudley village on a long, hot summer's day
And do you see old 'Cobblers Row' and small boys at their play?
No videos or pocket radios then, no expensive electronic toys,
A few marbles and a home-made bow were enough for those little boys.
We chased Indians around the 'Spuggies Hut', by the pit wall we
                                                            slew the Japs,
We killed Germans down the 'Garden Walks', (we were ferocious
                                                            little chaps).
Look back my friend, now look again almost fifty years or so
As two teenage lads out in the fields watched the seasons come and go.
We knew where the fox was lying up, where partridge nested in the hay
And saw wild ducks come flighting in at the end of the day.
Look again my friend, look back again forty years to those far-off days,
With early manhood and married life, our paths went separate ways.
Look back, my man, ten years or so, family's now grown and flown
                                                            the nest
And though we are both grandparents now, our friendship has stood
                                                            the test.
Good pals we've been, both man and boy for years nigh on three score
And my greatest wish, my dearest friend, is that we'll see twenty more.
Then when we are old and in our eighties, once again we will look back
And talk about things we have seen and done
                    Now *that* will be some crack . . .

David F Jobson

STREETS OF OLD

I woke up this morning and couldn't believe,
The sights in my dreams I had seen!
I'd gone back to my childhood, a long time ago,
And relived the times that had been.

I saw roads and streets uncluttered by signs,
Like 'no parking, one way, stop, go slow'.
And the pavements were free, no meters to see,
Or warnings and strict threats of fines.

Everything looked old fashioned and quaint,
No cars roaring by really fast.
No lines of yellow, prohibitive paint,
All this is my dream of the past.

No 'humps' in the road, to slow traffic down,
No roundabouts, mini or major!
The scene was the same in village and town,
Tranquil! With no hint of danger.

And it didn't stop there, as I took time to stare,
The houses were just as you'd wish,
Lovingly maintained with infinite care,
With no sign of a satellite dish!

Time doesn't stand still! Would that it will,
But the visions seen there in my sleep,
Will stay in my mind and future dreams fill,
The images there, mine to keep.

Jack Wilkins

My 5-Barred Gate

How I loved that 5-barred gate,
I used to swing on
When I was eight.

It was old and weathered
And the hinges would creak,
It gave me such pleasure,
I could hardly speak.

It shuddered and rumbled
As it rubbed on the ground,
As to and fro I went,
How I loved that sound.

But now I am older,
I'm resigned to my fate,
I wonder if Heaven
Has a 5-barred gate.

Edna Gosney

MILLDALE

I had a favourite place I'd go, down by a stream
Where I used to go just to daydream
The wild rhubarb by the babbling brook
Bouncing over each pebble, cranny and nook.

The little stone bridge is no longer there
As a child I'd play 'Pooh sticks' just like the bear
A kingfisher darts by with a flash of blue
Up in a tree two doves bill and coo.

Buttercups and daisies nod their heads in the breeze
Telling the time blowing dandelion seeds
Summer walks with the dogs up by the lake
Bonfire Night, putting potatoes in the oven to bake.

Winter in those days had lots of snow
The snowmen would just grow and grow
These childhood memories are precious and mine
Of when I was about eight or nine!

Wendy Rennison

CHILDHOOD ILLNESS

Your mother's just gone down the shops
to buy a bit of bacon
and for your father two lamb chops
then the dinner she'll be makin'
She baked a cake this afternoon
it's chocolate, and some stotties
she had to bake some extra bread
to take to Auntie Lottie's
She's home from hospital the day
and Uncle's gone down by
he can't afford to lose the pay
with Christmas drawin' nigh
Your brother Billy's home from school
I've sent him for a bath
he got into another fight, by!
he'll face your mother's wrath
Cousin Moira says she's gone
and passed her eleven plus
so Auntie Jean's put out the flags
eeh! she's makin' such a fuss
Granma's gone to Newcastle
to do some Christmas shoppin'
she'll just get fraught and flummoxed
then come home and say she's droppin'
Granda's at the allotment
he's gone to do a deal
he'll swap some veg and flowers
for a duck, for the Christmas meal
And me, I've just been sittin' here
darnin' your old socks
watchin' over you, while you're
in bed with chicken pox.

Mary Younger

CHILDHOOD MEMORIES

At home we did our daily tasks,
Life was so honest, there was no mask;
We walked to school through narrow lanes,
If misbehaved, we got the cane.

We raised our hand to question Sir,
We sat in desk without a stir;
We learnt our tables off by heart,
We said our prayers when day did start.

The roadman kept the verges neat,
He dug the ditches throughout his beat;
The policeman walked from street to street,
He won respect from those he'd meet.

No sign of telly or mobile phone,
We went to butcher to beg a bone;
At village shop we had our treats,
Half of a penny to buy some sweets.

Just once each year Dad took a break,
We walked to Halt, a train to take;
One long, whole day, to play on sands,
Punch and Judy and music from band.

To Sunday School we went each week,
To the hedgerows, a bird's nest to seek;
On Sunday night when work all done,
Together the family walked for fun.

We played our games on village pitch,
At home, dear Mum, our clothes did stitch;
The standards needed for future life,
Were all ingrained, no sign of strife.

John Paulley

THE WINDMILL

Oh, picturesque mill, how spirits soared!
Oh, what a gem, so faithfully restored!
Harking back to a rural life, seldom bliss,
Recalled as if something we now miss

The majestic sweep of wheeling sails
Relishing stiff breezes, ducking the gales
How do mills cope with such fickle wind?
You trim your sails, the miller grinned!

In harnessing the wind's turbulent power
To turn great millstones and so grind flour
One cannot help but admire the skill
Of the craftsmen who built the mill

Come inside, see ladders to circular rooms
Hear the mill-shaft's thunderous booms,
The gear-wheel, as it judders and creaks
Meshing teeth, made from hardest teaks

Round and round rumble millwheels of stone
Feel wooden beams vibrate and groan
Trap doors open and clack shut again
Announcing the hoist of each sack of grain

Rushing grain feeds gnashing stone jaws
While hard manual work on other floors
Freshly ground flour spews down a chute
Into white woven bags, made from best jute

Wind's eased, we'll close the mill for today
Sadly, the late arrivals will be turned away
To learn more about how things used to be
Tomorrow, it's fresh bread and cakes for tea

Derek Harvey

THE AUTUMN OF LIFE

As we grow up and we start to grow old
We think about things as children we were told -
Like the day we went by steam train down to the sea
My mum, my dad, sister and brother and me -
Sitting by the fire with our thoughts running wild
And look back over the things we did as a child -
There were games like five-stones, spinning tops and conkers
Tell our children about it today and they think you're bonkers -
When we went to the pictures and bought a tub of ice cream
If we saw Dracula or The House of Wax, it really made you scream -
How exciting when you met your first boy or girlfriend and thought
                                                        you were lovers
I'm sure it was more exciting keeping it a secret from our mothers -
Those thoughts we can treasure as we get old
And think of the best bits as our life we unfold -
Perhaps now that we have a partner, husband or wife
No matter what, they can help us enjoy the autumn of life.

Eddie J Owers

HOXTON

1938 in Hoxton, London, I was born
Everyone was very poor; our clothes were old and worn
We had no shoes upon our feet, no jewellery or toys
Just lots of scruffy, rough and ready, happy girls and boys
Then Hitler reared his ugly head and friends began to die
The searchlights and the doodle bugs filled our English sky
Friends and loved ones went to war, some never to return
Jews were brutalised and killed, will they never learn?
Then happy times returned again and hearts began to mend
Neighbours pulled together to help our bombed-out friends
We sat upon our doorsteps and passed the time of day
And anyone who sauntered past, went merrily on their way
We had no cars or TV, no furs or diamond rings
Just friendship and the pleasures that simple life can bring
Front doors would be left open for neighbours to pop in
We'd brew some tea and share our woes and take life on the chin
Oh Hoxton, my dear Hoxton, will never be the same
The playgrounds and little streets are gone - it gives me so much pain
To see the park where we once played, where the flowers have been
                                                                    slain
Don't people care for simple things that used to give us joy?
The Hoxton as I knew it then has sadly been destroyed.

Rose Rands-Horscroft

A SUNDAY AFTERNOON WITH GRAN

I remember when I was four years old
Watching my gran in her apron bake
Her wonky, thick pastry jam tarts
And her 'famous' coconut cake.
That was a Sunday afternoon with Gran.

When I was five years old I recalled
My gran showing me how to knit
Clickety-click went her needles
In wonderment, with her I'd sit!
That was a Sunday afternoon with Gran.

At the age of six years old, I remember,
We'd play cat's cradle with wool
My gran was always a winner at this
Knowing exactly which string to pull!
That was a Sunday afternoon with Gran.

At seven years old, I can still recall
Gran's garden with me sitting alone
On a massive pebble, hidden under trees
It was Gran's special 'wishing stone'.
That was a Sunday afternoon with Gran.

At the grown up age of eight years old
With my cousin I'd hide under the stairs
Gran made us our 'secret den'
With her woollen blanket and chairs.
That was a Sunday afternoon with Gran.

The years have rolled by and I've grown up
But the stories I still love to share
Of my dear Gran with her apple bag bloomers
Rosy cheeks and wispy white hair.
So here are my memories of a Sunday afternoon with Gran!

Louise Mawbey

OLD FAMILIAR STREET

I think on my childhood, the days of shillings and pence,
when cars were Austin and Morris, and people more content.
We lived in communities where no one locked their door,
the postman called morning and lunch, and a third time at four.
Police boxes on pavements, and constables walking the beat,
the community slept easy, down on Old Familiar Street.

I think on my childhood, the days of inches, feet and yards,
when men like Winston Churchill were our heroes and stars.
We lived in communities where neighbours cared much more,
'Can I get your washing in? Anything you want from the store?'
A gentleman opened the door for a lady, and gave up his seat,
the community seemed at ease, down on Old Familiar Street.

Keith Leese

DOWN MEMORY LANE

Of all our gifts, perhaps the most,
Memories of days gone by.
Recalling those quite simple things,
Concerning you and I.

In time of quiet solitude,
Recalling long ago,
When memories come flooding back
Ecstatically, or slow.

When we were children, happily,
Enjoying every day,
Without a single worry,
In a world, just made for play.

The growing up, the time that flew,
Or simply passed us by,
Forgotten days, hard to recall
No matter how we'd try.

And then the lovely memories,
The first job, first romance,
When all the future stretched before
Like some exotic dance.

New families, horizons stretched,
New homes, locations, life.
The beautiful remembered days
When we were man and wife.

That dimly lit delightful lane,
Today, though not so clear
Is with us yet each faltering step
Becoming yet more dear.

Remembering, trying as we must
Straining our poor recall
Of that great gift, whose fading glow,
Returns to haunt us all.

Leonard T Coleman

NIGHT-TIME MEMORIES

When I was just a little girl
How I wished the wind would stop
Making awful noises
Through the chimney top

Blowing all the branches
Of our apple tree
Leaving ghostly shapes at night
Oh dear, how they frightened me

No longer just a little girl
I lie here all alone
I like to listen to the wind
It reminds me so of home

For nothing there would hurt you
Mum and Dad were always there
You always knew, they loved us so
Showing just how much they'd care

Susan Goldsmith

A VILLAGE NEAR PETERBOROUGH 1930S

The focal point was the Parish Church
With a yew tree and a tall birch
Down the main street, about a mile long
There were six pubs and a fire station
Also two schools and a village hall
A smelly river and an over-fall
Four bakeries and three grocery shops
Two butchers and three fish 'n' chip shops
Two barbers where men discussed the news
A large shop selling boots and shoes
A newsagent selling papers and magazines
Also selling tins of peas or baked beans
Five shops selling chocolates or sweets
We could pick and choose, where we got our treats
Three chapels, about a quarter of a mile apart
I should have mentioned right at the start
A railway siding where farmers loaded potatoes and beet
At harvest time this was a very busy street.

Rustic George

CHILDHOOD MEMORIES

Although I'm only 25
I have fond memories
Of things I did when I was young
Like climbing through the trees

Playing catch out in the playground
And kerbie in the street
And not having to be wary
Of every stranger I did meet

The drama plays I did at school
The costumes I had to wear
When I look back at the photos
They don't half give me a scare

A little secret meeting place
I had down in the park
Where all my friends and I would meet
But leave when it got dark

The first time I rode my bicycle
Without the stabilisers on
My mum promised she was holding me
But that was just a con

The day I touched the iron
To see if it was hot
And the day I fell into some thorns
Are days I've not forgot

My age is only 25
As I have said before
I have so many memories
And hope to have so many more

J L Preston

HAPPY LANDINGS

Remember the sledging?
The thrill of the spill?
The long trudge afterwards,
Back up the hill?
Wasn't it fun
Out there in the snow,
Smiling and laughing,
Our faces aglow!
Hoping and praying
It would not go away
So that we could go on
Playing in the snow.

R Vincent

TELEVISION

For us in the west to have television
Was truly a very momentous decision;
For nobody'd bought one just after the war
And they hadn't been marketed so long before.
But we wanted a set for the Queen's coronation
Which was being transmitted to all of the nation.
So we bought a TV set a few weeks before,
And I thought I had never enjoyed myself more,
It's funny what happens to somebody's mind.
I'd thought Messrs Churchill and Attlee quite kind;
But when I'd paid heed long to that television
I did not know this any more with precision:
And not only past leaders the TV did mock,
But its comments on current ones gave me a shock.
I hated that odious word 'Politician',
But I knew I did not hate of my own volition,
For it was the medium of television
That held up our leaders to constant derision.
But now television declares its intention
By showing us what we may prudently mention.
Cold water is poured on each common sense notion,
And at several others there's quite a commotion.
Doctors, lawyers, TV stars seem all in collusion
To bring us poor people to total confusion.
Television surely was not brought to our nation
For use as a method of indoctrination?

Jillian Mounter

Do You Live In Lapford

Did you live in Lapford, come from Nymet or from Bow
When you went to Jenny's drama classes, all those years ago?
When the course was over, you took her to one side,
Said if she'd go away with you, your love would all provide.
    Do you live in Lapford still?
    Are you Jack or Frank or Will?

Jenny told me later how she'd turn you down,
Said to go on acting, not to be a clown.
Did her refusal ruin you, embitter all your life?
Or are you my next-door neighbour, with a business and a wife?
    Do you live in Lapford still?
    Are you Debbie's Uncle Phil?

Did you work for the Ambrosia, in the office or the yard?
Were you the station porter? Are you now a guard?
Lapford actors stared up. For several years they ran.
Were you the chap behind them? Were you the leading man?
    Do you live in Lapford still?
    Are you the one that married Hil?

Had you raped the vicar's daughter? Were you getting worse
                                      and worse?
Did you then become a teacher? Very staid and very terse?
Were you already old, abandoned, in the lurch?
Have I been to your funeral, in the chapel or the church?
    Although I live in Lapford now, I think I'll never know
    If you are in the village still, or in Nymet or Bow.

Irene Tester

A CAREFREE 1970 SUMMER

Lazing in the sun listening to 'Spirit In The Sky'
Life was carefree and good as in the sun you'd fry
No worries in the world, a transistor by your side
A tie and dye grandad shirt and flares oh so wide

Walking to school with the latest LP under your arm
Spud-picking, back-breaking work on Gillmore's Farm
The only way to earn some money to get something new
We thought we knew what life's about, we hadn't got a clue

Playing football all day long in the park
Changing to kick the can when it got dark
Knocking doors and running away, trying not to get caught
Cos if caught, a lesson you'd be taught

Scrumping lovely Victoria plums, apples and pears
Being a schoolboy non-conformist, having very long hair
Bird-nesting, shooting tin cans with a catapult
Funny but if things went wrong it was always my fault

I wouldn't change a thing, it really was that good
I'm glad it turned out okay cos you only get one childhood
Restrictions on children nowadays really ain't no fun
1970 was a carefree time bathed in lovely golden sun.

Leigh Smart

DRIVING IN MALTA

When visiting Malta - I've found,
    The visit just isn't complete;
Without a car to get around,
    It helps to save the feet!

When driving in Valetta,
    In daytime, or the dark;
Things really are no better,
    It's difficult to park!

The Maltese have these buses,
    In yellow and in red;
Which pull up - causing curses,
    When passengers they shed!

In Malta, while driving,
    You'll find - if you're good;
That you chance of surviving,
    Depends on your mood!

Drive smoothly - don't hurry,
    As Maltese people do;
Stay calm and don't worry,
    Be one of the few!

This island of Malta,
    Is not big in size;
Just don't be a defaulter,
    Peace of mind is your prize!

Then back here in Britain,
    You're happy to know;
That in Malta, those smitten,
    Have nowhere to go!

R Bissett

HAPPY TIMES

A happy memory of my friend and I,
Playing on her swing boat, going so high.
Dressing up as doctors and nurses,
With other friends with scratches and bruises.

Sunday was a very special day,
All dressed up in our glad array.
Going to Sunday school, singing choruses,
Learning our prayers and what Jesus did for us.

When I got home my job would be,
Walking to the allotments, feeling free.
Getting my rhubarb and sprays of mint,
To finish the Sunday lunch off with content.

Sitting all together, a big family,
Eight of us together so happily.
A few basic things may be for some,
But a happier childhood for me couldn't be done.

Evelyn M Harding

ACTIVE CHILDHOOD

Some children these days are obese,
Lack of exercise, too much grease,
We lived on rations, but ate enough,
Grew up healthy, grew up tough.
On our bikes we rode for miles,
Ran over fields, jumped over stiles,
Walked to school in all weathers,
With our friends, altogether.

Our childhood days were lots of fun,
Full of action, every one.
School playgrounds were always busy,
Running round till we were dizzy.
Strenuous handstands against the wall,
Our favourite pastime, playing ball,
Skipping ropes, we all owned one,
An idle child? There were none.

Very few toys came our way,
So imagination came into play.
Up on stage, singing sweet,
With Mum's old shoes upon our feet.
Her dress, too long, dragged on the ground,
As we jigged and danced round and round.
We felt like queens in this array,
A treasured memory to this day.

Slid down haystacks, although forbidden,
Leapt over haycocks, truth was hidden.
Fed the rabbits, walked the hound,
Helped round the house, jobs were found.
We had discipline, but fun always,
In the 1940s, my childhood days.

Doreen Kowalska

NEW WORDS FOR OLD

Why be coy about your age?
It's more than just a date,
The words you use, the terms you choose,
Will set the record straight.

You may think life's been good to you,
Your mirror says 'you're great!'
But if you want to move from home,
You have to 'relocate'.

In times gone by, a 'town house',
Was a 'terrace' in a row,
Flats now are 'dwelling units'
Up and down in lifts we go.

To make a contact swiftly,
'Surf the Internet', how classy!
'Visit the Website' with 'fax and E's'
To telephone is passé.

Look into any pram these days,
With a 'coo' and a smile that's merry,
It won't be an 'Arthur' or a 'Gladys' there,
But a 'Sharon', a 'Wayne' or a 'Kerry'!

So be brave and true and forthright,
Don't be slow to state your years,
So much can give the game away,
Much more than first appears!

So give your 'best shot', 'at the end of the day,'
And on these facts contemplate,
In fifty years' time from now all this
Will be well past its 'sell-by date'.

Elizabeth Rapley

MEMORIES

Memories, times passed by,
Some are sad and make me cry,
Others happy and make me gay,
Memories make me feel that way,
Young lass played all day,
School I'd make my way,
Miss Butterworth, a favourite teacher,
Mr Wright, the district preacher,
Education was my goal,
Wisdom started to unfold,
Knowing more about life,
Husband, children, now a wife,
Children, adults, left the nest,
Knowing all, still Mum knew best,
No marbles, now computers and PlayStations,
Fortunate not to encounter drugs,
A friend happened to get mugged,
Iraq, Saddam Hussein is the topic,
War, people disagree, wishing to stop it,
Mr Blair and Bush adamant to rid,
Terrorists and illegal weapons,
Debates in the House of Commons,
War some take delight,
Why do they need to fight?
Memory, World War II, lasting six years,
Under the stairs I said my prayers,
Manchester glowing, bombs, a bonfire,
Memory repeated I do not desire,
Memories wrote in rhyme,
Implanted in my brain to the present time.

Alice Harrison

NIGHT-TIME MASTERPIECE

Jack Frost came to visit last night
With his calling card, what a wonderful sight
The intricate patterns on the windowpane
Unique every time, not one is the same
Today's double glazing, too warm to stay
He only needs the cold to be able to play
Canvasses were plenty in bygone years
Now he scans the country almost in tears
No legacies to go down in history
By daylight they have melted so no one can see

Kay Astbury

THE FUTURE AND THE PAST

Standing at the window watching the world go by,
The years gently roll back, the memories slip out with a sigh.
Childhood years were special days overflowing with fun,
From snowmen in the winter to frolicking in the summer sun.
As the years came and went, disappearing quickly past,
I was determined to treat each day as if it was my last,
Researching the book of life-saving information for evermore,
Building a future, never knowing what was in store.

Leaving school and going to work was entering the unknown.
Faltering steps into adulthood, taking every kindness shown.
The carefree days were gone forever, responsibility taken on.
One September I fell in love, my days of loneliness forever gone,
Growing up together into adulthood until finally we were wed.
Those treasured vows of love still echo inside of my head.
Nine months further on our family began with a little boy,
Another three years passed before a daughter added to our joy.

The following years I spent teaching them everything I knew.
The children grew to adults, spread their wings and flew.
At first the house seemed empty with everybody gone,
Finding new things for two didn't take us very long.
Along the way grandchildren added to the family tree
And how I did enjoy the new role cast upon me.
As all children do, they're growing up so very fast.
Standing at the window I enjoy the future and the past.

Zenda Cooper

'OLD' TRURO

Of the Truro I knew, I often dream.
Where from every gutter there flowed a stream.
Cobbled streets and narrow lanes,
And cottager's cards in their windowpanes
Saying, *Vacancies*, come look and see,
Or *Won't you try our fresh cream tea?*
Tiny tea shops, bright and clean,
With copper pans of Cornish cream.
On hissing steam-drawn trains we'd go,
Perranworthal - Perranzabuloe.
Tiny branch lines - China day,
With Falmouth - not too far away.
A special treat - or glory be,
We'd catch the boat from Lemon Quay
On summer days we'd all set forth,
St Erth, St Ives or Perranporth,
With spades and buckets - oh what glee,
Then back to Truro, for our tea.
With Lardy cake and Saffron buns,
Cornish splits and Sally luns.
A candle lit our way to bed,
A goosedown pillow to lay my head
And wafting on a summer breeze,
The scent of blossomed apple trees.
Moonlit orchards - cathedral spires,
On winter nights, the cosy fires,
Star-studded skies, all diamond-bright
Would glitter on a frosty night.
Of the Truro I knew, I often dream
When from every gutter, there flowed a stream.

Hilda Jones

DOWN MEMORY LANE

When we were young, life seem'd at peace,
Hopscotch by day:
No thought this life would ever cease -
No more to play.

We went to bed by candlelight,
Till break of day:
Routine unvaried every night -
No other way.

Life was simple but full of fun -
TV unknown -
Roller-skates and tops that were spun:
Our life our own?

Ruth Shallard

CAPTIVATING

I read the words 'down memory lane'
Then there was I travelling on it again
How many times had I walked there
On that always busy thoroughfare
Babies in prams and tiny tots
Talk about children, school had lots
College with the teens and tutors
School bags now carried by six footers
Cars with 'L' plates back and front
All steered by the famous 'James Hunt'
Then there was the hand in hands
Stars in their eyes, head full of plans
Bridal car with 'Aisle Alter Hymn' rear
The confetti mob with intention sincere
Father, Mother, Granny and Grandad
Join with friends in a joyful jihad
Who is not captured by 'memory lane'
Where at this moment is your brain.

Sarah Smeaton

CAREFREE DAYS

A cottage in the country
In a wooded dell,
Sheltered from the north-east wind,
Our water from a well.

Here we spent our childhood,
And early teenage years
My younger sister and myself
Sharing hopes and fears.

A commotion in the hen house,
Would wake us in the night,
A hungry fox was on the prowl,
Hoping for a tasty bite.

Carefree days of fun and play,
In the fields and woods,
Tobogganing down the hillside
In winter snow was good.

After school we would stop
At the village forge,
Hoping for a horse to see,
Being shod by blacksmith George.

We climbed the stairs by candlelight,
Got quickly into bed,
Then listened to the hooting owls,
That rats and mice so dread.

All these memories and many more,
We still think of today,
Our carefree days of childhood,
Which seem like yesterday.

Lois M Pester

WINTER MEMORIES

White snowdrops with hanging heads
Lightness that illumes the beds
In the garden's winter cold
Memories of days of old

I see them as I did then
Snow carpet, thousand and ten
They stretched broad and yonder
Made my eyes wide with wonder

On the side of a mountain
Excitement I couldn't contain
Each day we walked among them
Try not to damage long stem

My heart filled with youthful love
Steps light; blue heavens above
Her hand held in mine, lightly
I squeezed hers more tightly

Taking her into my arms
Profound thrilling of her charms
Her scent came across in wafts
Our first kiss 'mongst the snowdrops.

Len Beddow

DOWN MEMORY LANE

My sister and I, when we were young
Were mad about cut-out dolls
We saved all our pennies for new ones
And couldn't wait for the hols
With them spread on the kitchen table
We would hold our own fashion show
It was our very special favourite game
And the hours never went slow
We had cut-out dolls of every kind
Some from history and nursery rhymes
Babies and families and glamour girls
And film stars of the times
Even our mother would join in our game
Which made two little girls content
Wonderful memories of times past
And the happy hours we spent.

June Davies

To Annabelle

See yonder willow on that bank, in graceful majesty;
Where as a lad I whiled away the hours of yesterday.
The sparkling brook beneath its spread, where lively fish displays;
The birds that from its boughs ring out, in all my yesterdays.

It's there I courted Annabelle, a lass so full of grace;
With laughing eyes, with golden hair and radiant of face.
Beneath that willow blossomed love, in summer's ripening haze;
The heart still tender with desire, for all those yesterdays.

Oh! Annabelle, dear Annabelle, now you have gone before;
The memories you leave me, I shall treasure evermore.
Where dragonflies on water dance, and rabbit comes to graze;
I yearn once more for moments shared, in all those yesterdays.

And when we meet again someday, and prove the doubters wrong;
We'll sit beneath that willow's shade, and hear the thrush's song.
Enjoy the fruits of summer, as we laugh and love and laze;
Reliving every peaceful hour, in all our yesterdays!

Merrick James

CHILDHOOD

My earliest thoughts are of a cobbled street,
Terraced houses, drab but neat,
That stretched in a long, long line,
That shrank as I grew with time.
A dog called Pal, a mongrel cur,
A lime-washed yard with chickens there,
Horses queued outside the door,
To be given spuds, though we were poor.
A little boy, wary, distrustful,
Proffers a spud to a huge toothful muzzle,
Minding his toes, in pumps, no socks,
From giant hooves with hairy hocks,
That struck the very sparks of life,
From cobbled stones, dead and dry,
Their swishing tails and tossing manes,
That seem to die when it rains.
The rain, the pools, the matchstick boats,
The hurried search for things that float,
Then the striving, the never-ending bid,
To stop them floating down the grid.

Harry Lyons

REMEMBERING

The deckchairs are stacked
The man has gone home
But who is that lady
Paddling in the foam?
Why paddle at this hour?
Hypnotised by the surf
Her feet on sharp coral
Why doesn't it hurt?

This little lady
She's old and she's bent
She is remembering
Times well spent
When she danced to sweet music
Her own 'String of Pearls'
Played on a saxophone
With her dress out in swirls.

Dorothy J White

TRIBUTE TO A COAL MINER

When I was lad things weren't all that bad
We didn't do much learning
Because we had to go out earning
On my first day down pit
An oil lamp was lit
As the coal face was hit
My body was a-burning
And my insides were a-churning
How I wished I done more learning

With the oil lamp's flame burning fast
I thought to myself, *how long can a man last?*
Then all of a sudden there was a big blast
I turned and saw canaries flee past
Would you believe they'd all been gassed?
By then us was all in a lather
Next thing I knew I was grabbed by me father
He shouted to me, 'Get up that ladder'
By then I could see me father get madder

Later that night we all went for a pint
This we needed to get over the fright
Me father said, 'What you've seen this night
Is an all too common sight'

And to count ourselves lucky
As we'll see the dawn light
Later that night as I lay in bed
I thanked the good Lord He saved my head

I tried to put my worries away
Cos I had to go down pit next day
In my mind that day will always linger
That is why I will claim for whitefinger

J Laverick

MEMORIES

I used to wish when the children were small,
That the days would be longer to do it all,
There'd be walls to paint, sewing to do,
Gardens to weed and loads of stew,
But the time passed so quickly and before I knew,
They'd grown just like 'Topsy' and out of the blue.
Our lives took on a different hue,
Now they have all gone their separate ways,
Life's days are longer, for me anyway,
No more gardens to weed and walls to paint,
Prams to push or bread to bake.
That's all behind me, seems selfish to say,
I do as I wish now, but miss the 'heydays' of
Parties and friends to stay overnight,
And Jane, who always said, 'Mummy is right,
Mummy says this, Mummy says that'
But it was Mummy who finally
Kicked out the cat.

Patricia Birmingham

YESTERDAY'S DREAMS

What now to do that the years have gone?
Where now to go on a journey long?
How will I find the dreams of my mind
Made in the days when young and blind?

To follow a memory that comes in the day,
Go back to the places found on the way.
Where dreams were made, where dreams were planned,
In a near or a far and distant land.

If I could return to one dream that I've seen,
So long ago now since I have been.
Perhaps I could find my lucky star,
Do you think I should go? It's really far.

Where have I been since my yesterday's dreams?
Where did I go? So short the time seems.
What have I done along the way?
Was it all a dream? I really can't say.

Where now the laughter, where now the fun?
Where now the endless days in the sun?
Where now the nights that never did end?
I ask you again, where now to my friend?

Mair Wyn Cratchley

LOOKING BACK

In the autumn of life, looking back,
To assess what we have to show,
Its years of changes, progress, memories,
All bathed in a golden glow!

Childhood when life was carefree,
The war, that changed it all,
Those dark days of uncertainty,
With heartbreak over all!

The following peace, changing,
A way of life as we knew it.
Altering every walk of life,
How did we ever get thro' it?

Telephones became commonplace,
Ever more planes in the skies,
Gadgets made life easier,
Shops had endless 'good buys'!

Television soon arrived,
'Hippies' were on the scene!
New technology every day,
Freedom in all its forms, reigned!

Then came space exploration
Men walked on the moon!
Horrific nuclear weapons,
To be on the agenda soon!

Now we live with technology,
Robots, machines have a place,
Gone the tranquillity of childhood,
Now it's survival we face!

Sometimes I wonder if progress is better,
Today there's no time to write even a letter!

E M Eagle

OLD AGE

Childhood memories, long happy days
Harvest festivals, Christmas plays,
Summer holidays, sea and fun,
Football, cricket, tip and run.

Middle-age came and went so fast,
Tomorrow's dreams now the past,
Plans for the future, long buried and dead,
Prayers unanswered, words unsaid.

Limbs much weaker, back bowed and bent,
No more trips out - incontinent,
Walking once a pleasure. Now pure pain,
Assisted by a Zimmer frame.

Evening falls, I'm quickly fed,
7pm tucked up in bed,
The nights are long, desolate and still,
Eerily disturbed by groans and dispensing of pills.

Four score years, what the hell have I done?
I suppose I must have had some fun,
Curtains drawn, I've made another day,
Thank you dear Lord, what more can I say?

Colin Clarke

THE LAMPLIGHTER

Clogs on the cobbles, the start of a day
The lamplighter's efforts to show them the way.
Six in the morning the whole world asleep
Except for the ones who had jobs to keep.
All streaming down from the Lancashire hills
Through the tall iron gates of the satanic mills.
Flat caps for the fellas and shawls for the lasses
The backbone of England, the staunch working classes.
Dyeing vats, winding frames, carders and looms
All standing proudly in different rooms.
The racket from these to the ears an abuse
And signs making words were forever in use.
With noon came the signal for all work to end
And children from school at the gates would attend.
Some carrying food wrapped in kerchiefs of red
And others with packets of freshly baked bread.
Then back to the grind and the warp and the weft
Yarn being joined up by fingers so deft.
Constant inspections by men at the top
Ensuring no system had come to a stop.
Wearing bowlers and watch-chains and fine waxed moustaches
To the prettiest girls they would sometimes make passes.
This was often unwelcome but everyone knew
No one ever said no to the management crew.
Six in the evening, the end of the day
And the lamplighter's efforts still showing the way.

Joan Whitehead

THE GAS-LIGHTER

The Gas-lighter would come at night
With his long, long pole
To light the hissing shadowy light
Outside the Village School.

He'd take his ladder on his bike
Down each darkened road
And pull the chain that lit the gas
To lighten each abode.

The lights were few and far between
They'd give an eerie glow
And shadowy figures you could see
Come crunching home on snow.

One of my earliest memories
Was of my Grannie by the bed
Kneeling to say her nightly prayers
And the gas-light through the window shining by her head.

For we only had our candles then
And oil lamps lit for tea
But the gas-light lamp in the street outside
Was lit for all to see.

Those were days of long ago
When I was just a child
The memories linger on and on
When all seemed meek and mild.

Mollie D Earl

THE STREETS WHEREIN WE ONCE DID PLAY

The streets wherein we once did play,
all belong to the past in yesterday.
We used to play happily, so wild and so free -
have all but become sadly distant, faded memories.

For you and I we never held such a care,
as to what lay ahead - as we were not aware.
Of what the future held, as all you and I saw;
where childhood fantasies: to us they meant more!

Of what we were to become, and we both dreamed we could be!
A footballer, soldier - yet could never really see.
Or ever did know if these dreams would come true,
at that time we held so dear; inside of me and you!

We only lived for today and left tomorrow to chance,
all that mattered was now - and as for circumstance!
We learnt by our own mistakes: although they were few!
But still being so young; neither you or I knew.

Until we were older and much wiser with time,
back then life to us was like a Christmas pantomime!
That to us was a game that could not ever end,
though to our own dismay - one day it did end my friend!

Echoes of childish laughter - still it rings in my ears,
all of those memories now replaced by sad, wasted years.
Of growing one year older: one foot near the grave,
and for those precious moments - herein my heart I do save;
longing so to be there through those times again!

I shall remember with fondness those streets where we played,
where as a child I grew; won't ever be way-laid.
To a dank and dark corner - somewhere in my mind,
for as I get older; I forever do find -
I am continued to be drawn to these memories in time!

Sean Michael Atherton

THE KINGFISHER

Back through the mists of memory,
Flashing across my sight,
Come the magic words, 'Look, a kingfisher!'
That most wonderful bird in flight.

In the 1930s when work was short,
My brother was almost a man,
I was only seven, just a little girl,
To make me happy would be his plan.

He'd give me a ride on his bike,
Meet me from school, we'd go where the blackberries grew,
On the edge of the wood were the mushrooms,
All their special places he knew.

I'm a woman grown, my brother's long gone
But I remember the kingfisher's flight,
I wonder if it shares his heaven,
God would not waste such a wonderful sight.

So, my brother, I thank you for the memory
Of flashing blue in a blue, blue sky,
Satiny mushrooms, blackberries wild,
And a world that was magic to you and I.

Hilary Mason

CHILDISH IGNORANCE

When I was just a little lad
My dad would make a simple toy
As a birthday or a Christmas gift -
And this, to me, was such a joy.

He would shape it out of wood -
A joiner was his trade.
Well-crafted, neatly finished,
It always made the grade.

I'd see him in our garden shed;
I'd ask what he was doing -
Working on that piece of wood -
But that was my undoing!

He'd stop what he was making -
He'd turn his weary head.
He'd say, 'It's a wimwam so that ducks can peek,
And why aren't you in bed?'

I didn't know just what that meant -
So I'd go and ask my mum.
She'd smile and say politely,
'One day, you'll know, my son.'

Brian M Wood

GOOD OLD DAYS

As children we could play outside,
Or we'd all go to the park,
We could go for walks across the fields,
Return back home as it got dark.

Nobody was worried much,
In those happy, carefree days,
We scrumped for apples, climbed the trees,
And made up games and little plays.

We played hopscotch, leapfrog, rounders,
Threw two balls against the wall,
Went sledging and built snowmen,
When the snow began to fall.

There wasn't any traffic so
We could ride bikes to the stream,
We'd paddle and catch tiddlers,
If we were lucky, buy an ice cream.

There was no TV or computer,
No McDonald's, not many toys,
When it rained we read and played Ludo,
But we were such happy girls and boys.

Now parents worry about their children,
Never let them out of their sight,
Fear of strangers and fast, speeding cars,
And no one can walk out at night.

Kids today don't seem content,
Watching videos and DVDs,
Designer clothes and mobile phones,
Computer games and the latest CDs,
They have so much more in many ways,
But I prefer the good old days!

June Melbourn

REMEMBERING YOU

I keep trying to write this poem
Though the words don't quite connect
There's so much I want to say to you
But it's not having much effect.

You were always there for everyone
Doing things with dedication and care
Never once complaining how you felt
But I know the pain was there.

Enriching our lives in so many ways
In all the memories you've left behind
I thank God I was able to share such joy
With a dad so loving and kind

The tears are getting fewer
I've got you locked deep in my heart
I pray one day we'll be together
And never more to part

I'm learning to look at your photo
And not to cry when I speak of your name
I can play music I couldn't before
But it will never quite be the same

Why does God take the ones we love?
I still don't understand - *why!*
Though they say 'time is a great healer'
And to 'trust in God' we must try

So, I leave you in God's loving care
Until we all meet again
My prayers are always with you
As I dream down memory lane

Trish Wright

BOUQUET OF MEMORIES

Bonfire smoulders and smoke curls to rise
To the icy grey of winter skies.
The rich dampness of newly dug ground,
Fragrance of trampled grasses around.
The tang of dark soot spread out by hand,
With clouds of dusty lime on the land.

These smells always remind me of my dad,
Good times in the garden that we had.
Now even that he has long gone,
There's a part of him that still lives on.

Warm soapsuds steaming on washing day,
Tasty roast of beef cooking away.
Cinnamon flavour of apple pies,
Tins of yeasty bread starting to rise.
Beeswax polish in the living room,
The sweet scent of powder and perfume.

In the essence of these things I find,
Reminders that my mum left behind.
Now even though she has long gone,
There's a part of her that still lives on.

Wherever I am, in any place,
These smells conjure up my childhood days.
I can sense the hairspray on Mum's hair
And the aftershave Dad used to wear.
The happy times we shared back then,
Close my eyes and I am there again.

I see Mum and Dad as clear as day,
Memories no one can take away.
But even though they are long gone
There's a part of them in me living on.

Gilly Croft

THANKS FOR THE MEMORIES

Remember when we went to Canterbury
That suitcase on the train was a bit of a worry
But I'm glad we made it in the end
And that I shared it with you, my best friend.

Remember that time we went to Settle
Bloody hell, that weather tested our mettle
Apples and carrots were shared on our walk
I still wish that those two donkeys could talk.

One time we were told at a hotel greeting
That Stratford races had an evening meeting
The old lady said that it was a must
You couldn't see our heels for the dust.

Tower Bridge, remember the tube
Packed in like an Oxo cube
But the hotel was nice and that river cruise
The tour bus, the food and plenty of booze.

Well where next I wonder, I know where I'm off
Call me a rascal, a scoundrel, a toff
But I'll stop for a moment to say to my wife
Thanks for the memories, same again in next life.

Charlie McInally

CHILDHOOD MEMORY

As I walked along the lonely lanes
I remembered my times as a child
The days with my father who'd tell wondrous tales
Of Toadie and Rattie, those colourful rogues

These characters they stood in my mind
He'd go on for hours with more to tell
And then I'd get tired and want to go home

I'd tell my mother of Father's great tales
And she'd say, 'Don't be silly, they're only short tales'
But oh how I miss those days gone by
To see my father, we had so much fun.

Wendy McLean

MEMORIES OF YESTERDAY

We hold memories of the past,
Of a home, of loved ones we have lost,
Of a place that is now an empty space never to be filled.
That was oh so long ago,
Now we live so far away.
It's never far from our minds,
It seems like yesterday.
There have been times when we feel sad
To lose the things that we once had.
Now we hold a sense of regret
But with memories like these, how can we forget?

Richard Mahoney

MEMORIES

Memory used to be to me
Something I heard of but could never see,
As I've grown older and worn away,
My memory changes with each passing day,
Where once it mattered if snow should fall,
It hardly matters now at all,
Where once the dawning of the day
Would bring a greeting of warmth and play,
There stands the emptiness of today,
Memories of smiles and silly faces,
Making calls and going places,
All is lost in the realms of time,
All is lost that once was mine,
To miss the things that a memory brings
Is to travel in time without safety or wings,
To subject a heart to warmth yet to pain,
Knowing time can never return again,
Are we sure it is memory that hurts in this way?
Was it really so wonderful and why do we pay,
With wounds that won't heal and scars self-inflicted,
And all of our mind's pictures so warmly depicted?
If memories are hurting then why do we try,
To relive a past and not let it go by?
We all know our answers and only to us
Is the pain always worth it and the hurt always just,
We all hold them dearly with pain or with joy,
On special occasions our thoughts to employ,
And when Christmas day dawns please spare me a thought,
Don't worry or tell me what I oughtn't or ought,
I'll be having my memories and more than a tear,
For one I remember so fondly and dear,
To me now a memory I hold in my heart,
The hurt and the pain will come and depart,
But sooner or later the heartache will go,
Time is a great healer and as we all know,

One day it will change and with it will bring,
Just a warm thought of friendship and an old golden ring,
But my memory will last and I know this for sure,
Change as it might it's alive and it's pure,
True love can fade but never can die,
We can push it in corners and allow it to lie,
So memory to me is my gift for this year,
I won't be unhappy or living in fear,
Just entwining with time and wearing a smile,
But fondly remembering all the while,
Memories of occasions and happier times,
When I was his and he was mine.

Susanne Fest

THE MILL

Leigh's Alder Mill has gone - I feel sad,
The Lodge too - where I fished as a lad,
The big, tall chimney - towering high,
Has crumbled now - echoing Dibna's cry,
Memories too of years long past,
Of weavers to work - as a siren blast,
Huge copper dome - high with pride,
Heaped on a wagon - for a long last ride,
Historians' relic - of industrial past,
Has gone now - forever,
Fly the flag - at half-mast.

Brian Whiteside

SCHOOLS

One day in 1878
A new school opened up its gate
To welcome all the little ones
Every daughter, every son.

Each day this gate was opened wide
To let the little ones inside
To play, to laugh, to sing, to teach
That dreams were not beyond their reach.

Outside this gate the mothers stand
Watching their children, surveying the land
Of the place they will spend their younger years
Filled with laughter and with tears.

Today in 1988
This grand old building shuts its gate
For the very last time to the little ones
No more daughters, no more sons.

Further down the road I see
Children laughing, filled with glee
Another gate stands open wide
To let the little ones inside.

This modern school will bring much joy
To every single girl and boy
If they work hard and do their best
The teachers there will do the rest.

Chris Mace

A Girl's Brigade Pal

Where are you now?
Half a century has passed.
Those years have flown
Much too fast.

I remember your smile.
We shared a lot of fun.
I never fully understood
Why you became a nun.

I heard they sent you overseas;
To work in a far-flung mission.
I grieved for your great sacrifice
But admired your tough decision.

Then your parents moved away;
And news of you was severed.
Life went on for me, of course,
But without you, lonely weathered.

I long to hear if you are well;
Of the things you have achieved.
The Lord just had to bless your life
Because I know that you believed.

I trust that you are in His hands
Under His 'eagle's wings'.
Down here, up there, or anywhere;
God bless you with many things.

Barbara Paxman

ELDERLY MINDS

Lost to a world of twisted images,
Covered in clouds of dusty confusion.
Dusty from an age when youth was on their side,
Now everything is just an illusion.

Illusion or not, to them it's reality.
They are living it now in their years of finality.
The hardships of war and childhoods of poverty
Are just as real now as they were back last century.

Loved ones passed on return to their thoughts
After lying there dormant, asleep in their hearts.
Resurrected when needed - their spirits alive,
Give their long-troubled days reason still to survive.

And when they are gone, they themselves will live on
In the minds and the hearts of their daughters and sons,
Giving help once again to the ones left behind,
An oasis in the deserts of their elderly minds.

Audrey Harman

THE VALUE OF FRIENDSHIP

Friendship is a thing of value,
In all the world's nations,
The saying we know, is quite true,
You can choose your friends, but not your relations.

As we grow older, our friends do too,
And as we go through the years together,
We share so much pleasure in all we say and do,
In fair or stormy weather.

The years go by, our friends seem more dear,
We feel in friendship we want to cling,
And when they travel far and near,
We look forward to hearing the news they bring.

They tell us of their grandchildren, and how they've grown so tall,
And of all the joys they shared each day,
We all have memories we like to recall,
And our memories with us will always stay.

Nancy Queate

HIDDEN GEMS

As a girl I travelled on the bus,
For few owned a car in those days;
At a top speed of thirty it would take us
Down narrow country lanes and byways.

At each village and hamlet it would pull up
And the passengers would scramble inside,
Oft having to stand for the bus was full up;
We didn't mind, we were glad of the ride!

Progress came and the volume of traffic was such
That those byways and narrow country roads
Couldn't cope. They were out of touch
With pantechnicons and other heavy loads.

So they bypassed those little havens of peace
In order to rectify the situation
Of stress and strain to their narrow streets,
But condemned them to virtual isolation.

The villages are still there of course,
Every one a little hidden gem,
And I have such feelings of remorse
That I no longer have cause to visit them.

Marlene Allen

CAN I CARRY YOUR BAG?

Back in the late forties when I was just a lad,
I pushed a handcart that was made by my dad.

I carried the holidaymakers' luggage when they arrived by bus
                                    and train,
In those days Morecambe was very busy, not many people
                              went to Greece and Spain.

There were a lot more lads doing the same job,
All of us out trying to make a few bob.

A large number of visitors came to Morecambe from Bradford,
                        Huddersfield, Leeds and York,
Some clambered into taxis outside the Promenade Station,
                            and others decided to walk.

I would say, 'Can I carry your bag? Where do you want to go?'
Quite a few people accepted my offer and some said no.

The taxi drivers waiting outside the station, they were not too happy,
Towards us young lads, some of them became a little bit snappy.

One day I pushed four heavy suitcases from the Promenade Station
                              to the Eastend of town,
I remember it well, my feet were aching and a family rewarded me
                              with a half-crown.

I did trips from Euston Road Station to Sea View Parade,
Around the corner from the Alhambra Theatre and Market Arcade.

Walking down the road towards the sea front I could hear,
The music of Victor Silvester coming from the Westend Pier.

Every Saturday morning I went to the Gasworks on Moss Lane
                              for a sack of coke,
Pushing my handcart back up Billy's Hill, it really was no joke.

Dave Birkinshaw

OUR CHILDHOOD

When the young of the village went out to play,
In summer or winter, in warm or cold day,
Those games that were played down through the years,
Often with memories bringing back the tears.

How often in summer we would rush to see,
If the tide was in at the big quay,
For we knew then it was full at the slip,
As grabbing a bathing suit, we'd go for a dip.

Some would dry off by the heat of the sun,
While those that could swim seemed to have most fun,
Doing the 'crawl' or the 'backstroke' from slip to quay,
And showing off for all to see.

Other days round the avenue for a game,
Of playing cowboys and Indians, still the same,
Or hide and seek, or just climbing trees,
And sure to go home with dirty knees.

Or climbing on the mountain, trying not to fall,
We would play for hours 'til someone or all
Decided it was time to go home for a meal,
So back on the road, as a turnip we'd steal.

Going to the beach to a favourite spot,
Where we would bathe, read a book, picnic or not,
Though some would have sandwiches, others just bread,
A bottle of water, or a hat for the head.

In the evenings for a walk, so often we'd dare
To gang up on one, and give them a scare,
All in innocent fun at the end of the day,
Those highlights as children as we went out to play.

Imelda Fitzsimons

To The Loo At Ninety-Two

I just made it in time to the loo
'Tis not easy when one's ninety-two.
I'm sure you will all agree won't you?
But with legs unsteady I managed to wobble
I can assure you, it wasn't a bobble
And with a sigh of relief, by golly,
Everything was alright, oh! How jolly.
So proud was I of such success
I wanted to tell, I must confess.

Now the moral of this story, I relate,
Is never ever think there's time to wait.
Go straight away, when the warning you get,
Or I am sure you will truly regret,
Not heeding advice from an old hen.
So, all you people take heed once again,
From she who just reached in time, her throne,
In this situation, I surely can't be alone.
Please take heed, don't make a mistake,
Perhaps turning your bathroom into a lake.

Isabella M Smith

THE OLD FASHIONED CHRISTMAS

Give me the old fashioned Christmas every time
In our youth it was for us kids 'fine'
We waited for Father Christmas to come
Down the chimney bring toys for some
But we were told that if we did not go to sleep
Father Christmas would not come, we used to peep
Out of our bedclothes to see if Santa had arrived
In the end we were fast asleep, toys were supplied
A Christmas stocking with an orange, an apple, a coin, yes
Father Christmas had come in the night, God bless
We knew why we celebrated Christmas, it was Jesus' birthday
Jesus was born in a stable, no room at the inn, he did play
A large part in our young lives, that I just Tom do say
Christmas morning was for us said kids, then the evening
Was for the grown-ups, you can bet on just that
Beer and wine would be drank, oh boy, that was folk fact
What memories of our time at Christmas time of the year
Wishing everybody a happy, yes, for Christmas and new year cheer

T Sexton

THE MAN IN THE CORNER

Don't laugh at the man in the corner who comes in
on his own for a drink,
he sits by himself, looks up at the wall and seems to do nothing
but think;
he must have a home and a family, but nobody knows who he is
he slowly strolls in with his paper and sits with his pint and the 'quiz'.

Don't laugh at the man in the corner because he is sitting alone
he used to come in almost daily and meet with his friends
in 'their zone' -
they would sit and just chat about horses, or politics, or the big fight,
then all go back home feeling better having put the whole world
back to right.

Don't laugh at the man in the corner, he has lost all his friends
one by one
and although he was by far the oldest, he is left, and they have all gone;
today he seems even deeper in thought, surely someone will
go up and speak
shall I go? No - not now, I am late - maybe later on in the week.

Do you remember the man in the corner when he was left sitting alone,
no one went to chat, or pass the time of day although he was
all on his own;
he will never again take his favourite seat to meet his last friend
he has gone,
what a pity that nobody went for a chat, he had no one - wife,
daughter or son.

Jim Pritchard

IN DEAR FRED'S SHOP

When I recall was just the same as 'open shop'
Before almighty calm and woe
No bell ringing, few kids singing,
'Open up, it's nearly school!'
Banging window - never cool -
'We've pence to spend -
Let's make and mend -
So sorry - now
We caused the row -
Just Friday teatime - in our joy
We bashed around - upon shop's ground
And then, what sin
We never thought
To place our litter
From lads' lollies in the bin!'
Business:
'Cannot start -
Cannot stop!'
- Then when it was five - we kids just dived
Out of shop's door
For 'footie-free' on village patch
Now rough and bare - so for the time rare,
There was no 'shop scare'
You could see bare shelves
From gangs of elves -
Business *'Could not start, could not stop'* -
In dear Fred's shop!

Jac C Simmons

WARTIME REFLECTIONS 2003

Was it only yesterday
That World War II was underway?
And teachers' spoken golden rule
Was 'bring your gas-masks to school'?

Could it be but minutes passed
Since brave men fought and breathed their last
In foreign lands and raging seas
Whilst women wept on bended knees?

Memory speaks of tanks and guns,
Of widowed wives and fatherless sons,
Of shattered lives in more ways than one
As homes collapsed 'neath bombing-runs.

It speaks of towns wreathed in fire
Of dust and rubble and crushed desire;
Of children torn from mothers' arms
And moved to safer country farms.

It was a time as I recall
Of stripping curtains from the wall
To supplement a clothes short-fall,
And food rationing was hard for all . . .

Of land-girls working in the fields
To increase our meagre yields,
Whilst brave armies saw us through
On a diet of courage and bully-beef stew.

But, was it not in fact *today*
We heard of troops being sent away
To combat threats of poisoned air
Prompting gas-masks to reappear?

How come then, in this New Age
War *still* looms centre stage?

C Warren-Gash

TIMES PAST

When I was young the stars shone bright
Winking and twinkling through the night.
And nowadays they still shine on
Yet all their lovely romance has gone.
The moon as well has lost her shine
As lovers in her rays entwine.

When I was young, children could play
On beach, in fields or in woodland stray.
Yet now their parents keep them near
To home in their garden as they fear
That wicked people entice them away
And do them harm. It happens today.

When I was young, were folk so bad
As they seem today? Has the world gone mad?
Not so, for humans were always the same
Good, bad, indifferent, so what is to blame?
Perhaps it's because I am growing old
Or perhaps it's because nowadays we are told!

And so our world turns round and round.
Years go by and new things are found.
Yet the one who created this beautiful planet
May weep as He watches its deface
By men who were given it in care
To cherish and leave it for others to share.

Margaret Sleeboom-Derbyshire

REMEMBRANCE

Remembrance is essential
as forward we continue
in life experiential
of word and deed and venue

Recalling many moments
such as times we learnt to win
and failings and incidents
that we honestly call sin

Reflecting on the sorrow
how God helped us through the pain
gives us hope for tomorrow
seeing sunshine through the rain

Remembering the pleasures
many travels and delights
hearts blessed by retained treasures
thanking God for yesternights

Leslie C Gaston

SHAKE HANDS WITH A MILLIONAIRE

He bought me cherry lips
And a bag of coconut chips
He brought me crisps and pop
And then some sweet pit-props
(Can you still get them)

He taught me how to swim
But sometimes I wouldn't go in
(What a wimp)
And then to ride a bike
I had trouble staying upright

Come the summer holiday
We'd pack and go away
(Got the camera)
Two weeks by the sea
In hotel or B&B

He'd talk about the town
Ans we strolled around
(Called it his olden days)
And the things that I was told
Are worth more than a pot of gold

I've riches beyond measure
With the memories that I treasure
(Who needs a bank account)
Simple things done in style
Have always made me smile

There's one of us at play
A snapshot on a sunny day
(A legacy in an album)
No need for vintage wine
Ginger beer will do just fine

And as I stand at the sweet-shop door
I couldn't ask for more
(Well perhaps some rhubarb rock)
Dad put me on the path of life
Good job, sweet dreams, rich life

Val Stephenson

MEMORY

I remember, well I think I do
And then I go to see,
And it's never the way I thought it was,
Has it changed or is it me?

It's better never to go to look,
Your memories are precious to you.
Finding out they were rather different
Is not what you wanted to do.

So, sit in the chair and reminisce,
Remember your youth and your prime.
Remember it was all so easy then,
In the 'good old summertime'.

Now the thatch is silvered o'er
There's more memories than acts.
Still that means we have to remember less
When we try to give all the facts!

Joyce M Jones

PENFOLD'S GALLOPERS
(For David)

Penfold's Amusements have come to town,
Dance to the organ, let your hair down
'Roll up, roll up,' the showman cries,
'A penny to try the coconut shies.'

There in the centre of it all,
The magnificent carousel standing tall,
The proud Penfold owner calls, 'Come here,
Jump on, jump on, there's nothing to fear.'

Your father lifts you, high as he can
Onto a horse and pays the man,
Girls and boys all waiting there,
For the galloping horses at Penfold's fair.

You feel the rush of the wind in your face,
As your bright-coloured steed begins to race,
Hold onto his mane, let the reins go free,
As you dream of him frolicking in the sea.

The organ strikes up a festive note,
The breeze is tugging at your coat,
You hold on to your sailor's hat,
And give your charger a gentle pat.

Your little heart is beating fast,
Your horse is first . . . or is he last?
Ripples of laughter ring in the air,
Round Penfold's gallopers, heart of the fair.

The organ fades, the horses stop, teardrops fall and faces drop,
You cry and call your father's name, clinging to your horse's mane,
The Penfold man holds out his hand,
Your father sighs . . . and pays again.

Pam Penfold

MEMORIES OF YOUTH

I can remember the days that we sped
Penny on the tram to the old pier head
With bucket and spade, New Brighton bound
For one day of joy, pleasure unfound.

I can remember roads without cars
Tandems and bicycles, penny bazaars
Beef dripping butties, condensed milk in tea
Days in the country, fearless and free.

We didn't have much but we liked what we had
A night at the flicks or a dance made us glad
A boy on the arm and a hand-me-down gown
We were all set for a night on the town.

No one can know the pleasure we knew
Travelling by bus to the river at Kew
A glass of cider, some cheese and some bread
Relaxing with friends at the old 'Bull's Head'.

We had no telly and soaps were to wash
No sitting bored watching hours of tosh
We didn't have chat rooms, we talked to a friend
Hopes, joys and laughter for hours on end.

How could we know that a change was in sight?
War came our way like a thief in the night
Ration books, gas-masks and all of our joys
Calling up papers for all of the boys

So long ago, but fresh in the mind
Mothers and girlfriends all left behind
We made the best of the hardships that came
Knowing that life never could be the same

Joan Cooke

GRIEF

When it is winter
And the days are short and drear,
Sadness - like a tinter -
May dye a promising day dawn-clear
And rosy with the sun,
A threatening, darksome hue
And so lengthen one
Hour of true grief to two.

As each wintry day
Slowly runs its wintry course,
Maybe there's a way
Of remembering to endorse
Loss with fond images
Of the ones we mourn so that
Sorrow no longer damages
A natural peace of mind set

On seeing that this life is
Always part joy, part sorrow
As we hope to reach
The end at peace with tomorrow.

S V Batten

My First Teacher Miss Woodier

When I was at infant school about a hundred years ago
I fell in love with a lady there, I'm sure you'd want to know.
At night I used to dream of her, I'd do anything for a smile
Stand on my head, go head over heels, walk ten thousand miles.

She had jet-black, sort of frizzy hair, she was always kind and gentle
And even now after years have passed I still get sentimental.
She was my teacher, the best I had and I loved her really masses
She always wore a twin set and pearls and a chain to hold her glasses.

Miss Woodier was the teacher's name, she was young and very pretty
But I never told her of my love which really was a pity.
I always tidied up her desk, smoothed the cushion on her chair
When she was busy ticking books, I used to sit and stare.

Occasionally she would look up, and she would see me looking
'If you've finished all your work, come up and hand your book in'
I used to walk up to her desk, my heart would quickly beat
'Yes, that's very good, now go back to your seat'.

Each day she read us stories as we sat round her on the floor
Of wizards and kings and stressed out damsels and the knights
                                        of Elsinore.
The Secret Garden I loved so much, she always read so well
She the princess, me the knight, I'd slay the dragon in a terrible fight.

That was many years ago, now she is probably old and grey
But often I just think of her as she was in those distant days
You see, she will always look the same, there's no one to compare
With that teacher who I really loved with jet-black, frizzy hair.

Graham Perks

THE ROADS TO YESTERDAY

I love to linger on the road
that takes me back to yesterday,
I feel I'd like to share my load
with people who have gone astray.

To walk in paths I used to take
over hills, or by a lake.
See my footsteps in the sands
and mounds prepared by little hands.

Where squirrels live in nearby tree
and shake their shaggy tails at me.
Where hearts are filled in memory
of happy days that used to be.

To hear you laugh, to see you smile,
to walk with you a little while,
now I'm alone, I'd love to stray
along those roads of yesterday.

Andrew Dickson

ADIEU, ADIEU AND NOT FAREWELL

When I was but a little child
I heard with joy your infant cry
My brother who I loved so much
But now I weep and watch you die

I yearn for all the games we shared
While walking by our glittering stream
Alas our childhood days have passed
And vanished like a waking dream

But we had such different paths to tread
And often faltered on life's way
My love for you will grow not cold -
In distant realms we'll meet one day

My brother and my life-long friend
I can but say 'adieu, adieu'
The love we shared will never end -
Your care was constant, always true

Now I know your pain is past -
Our saviour brought you home at last.

Marcella Pellow

WAR YEARS
(1939-1945)

Fear was in everyone's mind in those years,
many grew weak and were often in tears;
during the war, many things we lived without,
rations grew tighter but we did not pout,
tightened our belts, went to bed early instead,
we cooked with dried egg, used all our stale bread
radio-recipes made sure families were fed,
we never had butter but used marg instead.

Gas-masks and ration books we all obtained,
mothers went hungry but never complained,
they made do and mended, over and over again;
turned curtains into rompers, or a dress for Jane.
Dyed rags and blankets to make fashioned coats,
used all kinds of paper for letters and notes;
saved bits of string and paper bags,
nothing was wasted, not even old rags.

'Put out those lights' the street warden would shout,
after tea, streets all dark and no one about,
as days dragged on, some gave up in despair,
we had to survive, rations we would share,
one egg was exchanged for a bit of cheese,
we had no extras in fridge or a deep-freeze;
one slice of corned beef, our week's ration of meat,
luxury of fresh fruit - a very special treat.

Neighbours were friendly, shared their grief,
an occasional letter gave some relief,
good news on the radio brightened our day,
bravely we carried on, there was no other way,
hidden within us was an unknown quality,
old people held together their family,
they sustained and strengthened daily,
their practical help was given constantly.

L Brown

REFLECTIONS

Now that I am old, I often sit thinking
Of when I was young and young girls were winking,
Wishing I was back chasing a chance,
Not giving my elders the glimpse of a glance.
My youth was wasted in my teens,
I dashed about full of beans,
Having fun and daring life,
Upsetting folk and causing strife.
The old ones said he's too big for his boots,
What did they know? Silly old coots.
For all their opinions I didn't give tuppence,
They frequently said I would get my comeuppance.
But now that I am old and think of those days,
Those old boys were right about my uncaring ways.
Now that I am old, a grey old codger
I spend most of my time as a coffin dodger.
But I spend some of my time keeping up to speed,
Not letting my mind go to seed.
How successful I'll be remains to be seen,
But on dodging the coffins I am still very keen.

Walker Ellis Williams

MEMORY LANE

To quietly stroll down one's own 'memory lane'
Most are good memories, while others bring pain.
How strange the things that trigger the mind
That sometimes make you feel fate's been unkind.

Your thoughts having strayed back into the past
Forgetting the blessings you have really are vast.
All those things you never had and friendships lost
Today's happiness, the price, yesterday's memories are the cost.

All those friends, the wonderful memories you hold dear
For many of those friends 'gone' now shed a tear.
Though they have gone ahead to prepare the way
For that next meeting of friends, 'a really special day'.

How wonderful all those special friends to recall
The blessings of those early years, yes, tears and all!
Those times that we shared, the good and the bad
All past, and them, makes one feel really sad.

By remembering them, they are still with us, all
Shed a tear by all means, but don't let it fall.
When we all meet again, in that place far away
Then hand them that tear, you saved till that day!

T W Denis Constance

MOM'S CAKE TIN

I'll always remember Mom's cake tin
Where it lay on the shelf, out of reach
It had pictures of kids playing leap-frog
By the pier on a warm, sunny beach.

There weren't any cakes in that cake tin
Only thru'penny bits, pennies and such
And with ha'pennies, farthings and tanners
It never amounted to much.

But it paid for those nice little extras
That help when you're down in the dumps
Getting over that grim influenza
Whooping cough, measles or mumps

Sheila M Smith

THE SOURCE OF LOVE

In the recesses of my mind are images
struggling to maintain their messages
for the substance of your life is elusive,
quick as silver to remain exclusive.
The memories of you, held in awe,
are beliefs treasured as never before.
The trust of your being to share
stirs each dawn of day in prayer.
Words formed by my lips are sincere
though others may poison your ear.
The hope for our love is revival
resting on truth of its survival.

Closing my eyes in concentration:
my esteem is without reservation.

Michael Alan Fenton